THE SHEPHERD

Dear Sebastian,

A MODERN PARABLE ABOUT OUR SEARCH FOR HAPPINESS

[signature]

MATTHEW KELLY

Beacon
PUBLISHING

THE SHEPHERD :
A Modern Parable About Our Search for Happiness

The Matthew Kelly Foundation
2330 Kemper Lane
Cincinnati, OH 45206
United States of America

First Edition published 2001.

Library of Congress Cataloging in Publication Data

Kelly, Matthew
        The shepherd: a modern parable about our search for
happiness / Matthew Kelly. - first edition
        ISBN 1-929266-07-3 (cloth.)
1. Christianity. 2. Spirituality. 3. Human Development.
4. Kelly, Matthew.
I Title

01 02 03 04 05 · 10 9 8 7 6 5 4 3 2

I would like to dedicate this book to
Amin Abboud.
You dropped a pebble in the pond
and the ripples have run to every corner of the earth.

Introduction

The human heart is on a quest for happiness. As individuals we are all so unique and different, but we are bound together by our common yearning for happiness. Regardless of our age or the color of our skin, regardless of the land in which we live or the land in which we were born, we all yearn for happiness.

In our search for happiness, we often do things that we think will make us happy, but in fact end up making us miserable. Under the influence of self-centered philosophies we often seek happiness through pleasure, possessions, power, or just simply the path of least resistance. Each of these may offer moments of happiness, but they end too soon, having lasted ever so briefly, and our quest for a lasting happiness continues. These moments of happiness are of course real, but only as real as a shadow is real. The shadow of a person is real and wonderful, but it is nothing compared to the actual person. Sadly, so many of us spend our whole lives chasing shadows of happiness.

The modern search for happiness seems to be governed by greed, lust, gluttony, selfishness, exploitation, and deception. And yet, as these diseased values become more and more the focus of modern lifestyles, people seem to be filled with greater discontentment and unhappiness with each passing day.

People don't wake up in the morning and ask themselves, "How can I make myself miserable today?" But at the same time, Henry David Thoureau's observation, "Most men lead lives of quiet desperation" has never held more truth than in this modern age.

At different times in our lives we consciously and sub-consciously put together a master plan for our happiness. We tell ourselves, "If I go to this college... and get this job... and marry this person... and buy a house on that street... drive that car... take vacation on that exotic island each year... and have this much money in the bank... then I will be happy."

Perhaps you have never put together such a comprehensive plan for yourself, but on a smaller scale we are constantly planning our happiness. Our hunger for happiness gives birth to the actions of our lives.

Once we have dreamt up our master plan we head off in the direction of this dream. For a month or a year, for five years or ten years we direct all of our time, effort and energy to the pursuit and fulfillment of our plan.

All of this leads to one of two scenarios that may seem very different, but in fact are very similar.

In the first scenario you devise your master plan, you pursue the plan, and you achieve the plan just as you imagined you would. After many years of putting together the pieces of your master plan, you finally wake up one morning and you have done everything you said you would do, and you have everything you wanted to have. You went to the right college, you made the football team, got the job, married the girl, bought the house, leased the car, vacationed on that exotic island, and saved that money for a rainy day… There is only one problem, you are still not content. Your yearning for happiness has not been appeased, the restlessness within you has not dissipated, you still feel there is something missing, you still sense there must be more to life.

Most people who find themselves in this scenario simply sit down and put together another master plan. This one is even bigger and better than the first. Then they spend the next ten years of their lives frantically chasing this new plan only to discover that their hunger for happiness is still not satisfied. And so it goes… they spend their whole lives chasing happiness… or shadows of happiness.

The other scenario is that you fail to achieve your master plan. You try to pull all the pieces of your master plan together, but it just doesn't work out. You direct all of your time, effort, and energy to the pursuit of the plan, but for whatever reason, it just doesn't come to fruition. You don't get into that college… she marries another guy… someone less qualified gets your dream job… and you get out-bid at the auction for the house…

This scenario can be even more tragic than the first, but not for the reasons you may think. The danger with this scenario is that we fall into a deep dark abyss of self-pity. Then, unless we are rescued by a new vision of happiness, we spend the rest of our lives telling ourselves, "If only I had received that promotion… if only I had a little more money… if only I had bought and sold those stocks at the right times… if only my master plan had worked out... then I would be happy!" There aren't many happy people in the land of "if only."

The great tragedy here is not that we fail to achieve our plan, but rather, that we don't know that even if our master plan had worked out, we still wouldn't have the happiness we desire.

We are fools to believe that we can find our happiness in these ways. Our master plans do not work. They will never satisfy the yearning we have for a happiness that is lasting and true. Whether our plans succeed or fail, the yearning goes on.

Fame, fortune, pleasure, and possessions will never satisfy our deep, deep yearning for happiness. Have you ever noticed that many people who are extremely wealthy seem unable to enjoy their wealth? They are always chasing more. Similarly, have you ever noticed that those who pursue pleasure as the ultimate end in life, whether through sex, drugs, alcohol, or food, likewise are never quite satisfied? They are always looking towards the next experience of pleasure. Possessions lose their glow in the same way. In the show room you can hardly contain the excitement over the new car you are about to purchase. But ten days, or ten weeks later, the buzz has disappeared. The car has assumed its place in reality as a means of transportation. The same is true of new clothes, or a new stereo, and thousands of other consumer products that we allow to consume us at different times of our lives. Are we still the consumers, or have we been consumed? We will never find a lasting happiness in fame, fortune, pleasure, or possessions. They are just illusions that sparkle and shine, and distract us from the true happiness we yearn for deep in our beings. The pursuit of pleasure and possessions as "ends" in themselves simply creates an ever-increasing desire for experiences and things that bring less and less satisfaction.

You never can get enough of what you don't really need.

Every human heart is on a quest for happiness, and our hearts remain restless until that yearning is satisfied. In every age and in every culture stories have been used to inspire and elevate people. This is a simple book. It is a storybook for adults and children. It is a variation of a story I heard some time ago, that touched me very deeply.

The Shepherd is a story about a man who has found the happiness that our hungry hearts desire. His simple and peaceful spirit provides a vision of happiness that is deeply rooted in ancient wisdom, but may just be that "new vision of happiness" that can rescue us all.

THE SHEPHERD

Once upon a time…

on a glorious summer's evening,
in an ancient English castle,
in the hills on the outskirts of London,
there was a banquet.

More than six hundred guests
had traveled from all over the world
to attend this lavish affair.

*There were movie stars and
musicians; artists and politicians;
princes and princesses;
fashion designers and beautiful models;
men and women who owned businesses
large enough to be small countries;
and a handful of others, of no particular note,
who had endeared themselves to the host
over the years.*

The evening was to be celebrated
not with music,
or speeches,
or dancing…

but with a presentation by a famous Shakespearean actor.

The people enjoyed a sumptuous meal and a wonderful selection of the finest wines the world had to offer.

The castle was radiant,
adorned with a springtime of flowers
and perfectly lit with a myriad of candles.

When the guests had finished their
dinner, but before dessert was served,
the host stood up and
welcomed his guests.

He then explained, "This evening, instead of music, and speeches, and dancing, I have invited one of England's most celebrated Shakespearean actors to perform for us."

*The people graciously applauded,
and the actor stood, moved towards
the center of the banquet hall, and
began to speak.*

He spoke eloquently and powerfully.

For thirty-five minutes he moved about the banquet hall, brilliantly reciting famous passages from the writings of William Shakespeare.

"Oh, I am but fortune's fool…"

"To be or not to be - that is the question:
Whether 'tis nobler in the mind to suffer
The slings and arrows of outrageous fortune
Or to take arms against a sea of troubles…"

"Shall I compare thee to a summers day?
Thou art more beautiful and more temperate…"

"…Neither a borrower nor a lender be, for loan oft loses both itself and a friend.

And borrowing dulleth the edge of husbandry.

This above all, to thine own self be true,

And it must follow as night follows day

Thou canst not then be false to any man."

After each brief episode the audience erupted in applause, and their applause echoed up through the castle and spilled out into the moonlit courtyards.

"'Tis but thy name that is my enemy:
Thou art thyself...
What's in a name? that which we
call a rose
By any other name would smell as
sweet;
So Romeo would, were he not Romeo
call'd,
Retain thy dear perfection which he
owes..."

"If we shadows have offended,
Think but this and all is mended,
That you have but slumbered here
While these visions did appear..."

With this, the closing passage from
A Midsummer-Night's Dream
the actor took a bow and
announced that he was finished.

The guests clapped and cheered and called for an encore.

The actor rose to his feet once more to oblige his eager audience.

*"If anyone has a favorite
Shakespearean
passage, if I know it, I would
be happy to recite it," he said.*

Several people spontaneously raised their hands.

One man asked for the soliloquy
from Macbeth.

Another for the balcony scene from Romeo and Juliet.

And then a young woman asked for
The Fourteenth Sonnet.

One after the other, the actor brought these passages to life - boldly, brilliantly, tenderly, thoughtfully - each excerpt matched perfectly with its corresponding emotion.

Now, an elderly gentleman towards the back of the banquet hall raised his hand and the actor called on him.

As it turned out, the old man
was a priest.

"Sir," he said standing in his place
to be heard, "I realize it's not
Shakespeare,
but I was wondering if you would
recite for us
The Twenty-Third Psalm."

The actor paused and looked down
as if he were remembering some
event far in the past,
perhaps a moment in his childhood.
Then he smiled,
and spoke up saying,

"Father,
I would be happy to recite the Psalm
on just one condition - and that is,
when I am finished, you too will
recite the Psalm for us here tonight."

The priest was taken aback.
He hesitated.
He was a little embarrassed now
and looking down he fidgeted with
the tablecloth.

But he really wanted to hear the actor recite the Psalm.

So finally,
he smiled and agreed saying,
"Very well."

The crowd hushed in anticipation
and the actor began
in his powerful and eloquent voice.

"The Lord is my shepherd,
there is nothing I shall want..."

When the actor finished reciting the
Psalm the audience rose to their
feet in ovation.
They clapped and cheered like they
would never stop clapping and
cheering, and their adulation again
echoed through the castle and
out into the midsummer's evening.

After several minutes,
the guests finally settled
and returned to their seats.

Then the actor looked down the
banquet hall to where the old priest
was sitting and said,
"Father, it's your turn now."

As the priest stood up at his table a whirl of whispers raced around the room.

Shifting in his place,
the old priest looked down,
placed one hand on the table to steady
himself,
and took a deep breath.

A look of vivid recollection came across his face. He seemed to slip away to some other place. Then in a voice that was gentle and deeply reflective, he began...

"The Lord is my shepherd,
there is nothing I shall want.

"He lets me lie down in green pastures.
He leads me beside peaceful waters.
He restores my soul.

"He guides me along the way of righteousness as befits his name.

*"Even though I walk through
the valley of the shadow of death,
I will not be afraid.*

"For the Lord is with me at my side.
His rod and his staff comfort and
protect me.

"He prepares a table for me in the
presence of my enemies.
He anoints my head with oil.
My cup overflows.

"Surely goodness and mercy
will follow me all the days of my life.
And I will live in the house of the
Lord, forever."

*When the priest was finished
not a sound could be heard in the
banquet hall.*

Nobody clapped,

nobody moved,

and nobody spoke.

A profound silence
had descended upon the castle.

Women wiped tears from their eyes.
Men sat staring open-mouthed.

A tear slipped from the eye of the host. And as the humble old priest gently sat down, every set of eyes in the banquet hall was fixed upon him.

The faces of the guests were covered
with awestruck amazement.

The actor was perplexed. He wondered why the priest's gentle words had touched the people so deeply.

Then like a shaft of light passing across his face, it dawned on him.

Seizing the moment,
the actor stood back up and said,
"My friends,
do you realize what you have
witnessed here tonight?"

They gazed back at him with a
communal stare of wonderment.
They knew they had witnessed
something profound, but were
uncertain of its meaning.

The actor continued…

"Why was the old man's recital of the Psalm so much more powerful than my own?

"As I see it -
The difference is this,
I know the Psalm,

"but Father,
he knows The Shepherd.*"*

Get to know The Shepherd.

Stop trying to put together
a master plan for your life…
for your happiness…

Instead, seek out The Master's Plan
for your life…
for your happiness…

Allow Him to lead you,
to guide you,
to be your companion,
your friend,
your coach,
your mentor...

He will lead you to green pastures…

He will restore your soul...

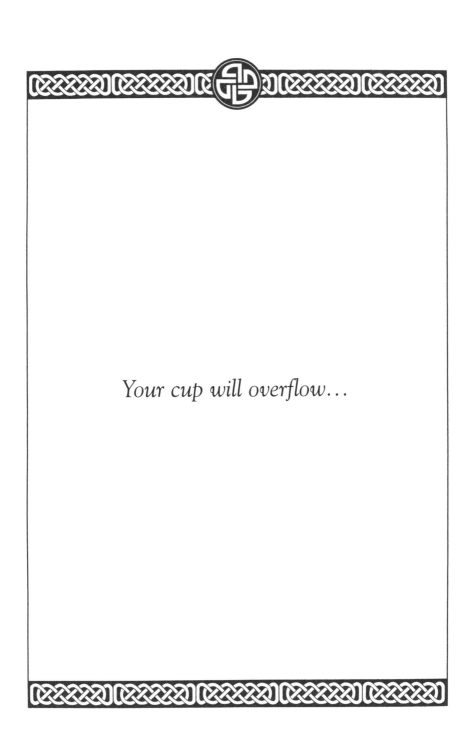

Your cup will overflow...

Afterword

The silent murmurings of my heart first captured my attention in a serious way almost ten years ago. At the time I was in college. Everything at school was going very well, I had a great group of friends, a wonderful girlfriend, and a good part-time job. On the outside everything seemed fine, but on the inside a growing restlessness was building up.

My heart was restless. I sensed something was missing in my life. I knew something was wrong, but I couldn't pinpoint it. I sensed there must be more to life, but I didn't know what it was, or where to find it.

I tried to ignore these feelings, but the nagging restlessness persisted.

Several weeks later I bumped into a family friend and he asked me how school was going. "Fine," I replied. He is a doctor, so he knows how to ask the right questions. For five or ten minutes he gently probed the different areas of my life. Each question and each answer led us a little closer to his diagnoses. Then he paused briefly, looked deep into my eyes and said, "You're not really happy, are you Matthew?"

He knew it and I knew it. I must confess I was ashamed to admit it at first. But our lives seem to flood with grace at unexpected moments, and I began to tell him about the emptiness and restlessness I was experiencing.

After listening to me carefully he suggested I stop by my church for ten minutes each morning on the way to college.

I listened, smiled, nodded politely, and immediately dismissed him as some sort of "religious fanatic." As he expanded on his idea and how it would transform my life, I wondered to myself, "How is ten minutes of prayer each day going to help me?" Before he had finished speaking I had resolved to completely ignore everything he had said.

In the coming weeks I threw myself into my studies, my work, and my sporting pursuits with more vigor than ever before. I had done this to appease my restless heart at other times in my life. But achievement in these areas no longer brought the fulfillment it once had.

One morning about six weeks later the emptiness had become so great that I found myself stopping by the church on the way to college. I crept quietly into the church, sat towards the back and began to plan my day. Just this simple exercise of planning the day ahead of me lifted the clouds of hurried confusion. For the first time in a long time I tasted a few drops of that wonderful tonic we call peace.

The next day, and everyday, I returned. Each morning I would simply sit towards the back of the church and move through the events of the day in my mind. With each passing day a sense of peace, purpose, and direction began to fill me.

Then one day as I sat there it occurred to me that "planning my day" wasn't really prayer. So I began to pray, "God, I want this... and I need this... and could you do this for me… and help me with this… and let this happen… and please, don't let that happen…"

For a few more weeks, this is how it went. Every morning I would stop by the church, sit towards the back, plan my day, and tell God what I wanted. For a while this was the depth of my prayer life.

And then, one day I had a problem. That morning I came to the church and with a simple prayer in my heart I began to explain, "God, I've got this problem… this is the situation, these are the circumstances… what do you think I should do?"

Asking that question marked a new beginning in my life. Up until then, I had only ever prayed, "Listen up God, your servant is speaking." But in that moment of spontaneous prayer the Spirit that guides us all led me to pray, "Speak Lord, your servant is listening." It was perhaps the first moment of honest and humble prayer in my life. Before that day I had only been interested in telling God what my will was, I had never asked Him to reveal His will.

"God, what do you think I should do?" I call this "THE BIG QUESTION." It is the question that changed my life forever, and the question that continues to transform my life today.

This question should be a constant theme in our spiritual lives. When we are attentive to this question we are happy regardless of external realities, because we have a peace and contentment within. It is the peace that comes from knowing that who we are, and what we are doing makes sense regardless of the outcome, and regardless of other people's opinions. This peace comes from taking into account the only opinion that truly matters: God's.

Everyday we make dozens of decisions, some of them large and some of them small. When was the last time you invited God into the decisions of your life?

I try each day to let God play a role in my decision-making. Sometimes I simply forget to consult Him. Sometimes I block His voice out because I want to do something I know He doesn't want me to do. Sometimes I foolishly believe that I know a shortcut to happiness. These decisions always lead me to misery of one form or another.Several months after I first began visiting our local church for ten minutes each morning, a very wise old man said to me, "You are unhappy. Think: 'there must be an obstacle between you and God.' You will seldom be wrong."

Several years ago I was on a plane just about every day and I got into the habit of writing one small passage each day. I would then use these passages to guide my thoughts, actions, and reflections for that day. A collection of those passages was later published as Mustard Seeds. My own search for happiness has led me to discover, "When you know you are doing the will of God, that alone is enough to sustain your happiness. When you don't have that, all the possessions in the world cannot sustain happiness in the depths of your heart."

The will of God is a mysterious thing. In my own spiritual journey I have learned that God reveals His will one step at a time, but this creates a great deal of uncertainty, and we don't like that. In this modern age we try to control all the elements so that we can have security and stability. If only we could learn to enjoy uncertainty. Uncertainty is a sign that all is well. God is your friend; He will take care of the details.

Our lives change when our habits change. My life changed when, encouraged by a friend, I began to pray for ten minutes a day. In those quiet moments of reflection I stumbled upon the big question: God, what do you think I should do?

For seven years I have been traveling around the world speaking to different groups of people. I cannot remember a time when I have not urged my listeners to enter into "the classroom of silence" for a few minutes of prayer and reflection each day. As these years have passed, more than a million people have attended my talks, seminars, and retreats, and sometimes I cannot help but wonder how many of those have actually formed the habit of spending a few minutes in prayer each day. Often people dismiss the message as too simple. It is true that the simple things in life are often the best. It is also true that simple things have a tremendous ability to transform our lives. Simplicity is the key to perfection. I have experienced the power of simplicity in my own life and I invite you to do the same.

So now it is your turn. Ten years from now, will this just be a nice story somewhere in the recesses of your mind, or will it be a book that has transformed your life forever?

Before you go to bed tonight, take a small piece of paper and write these four words on it: TEN MINUTES A DAY. Stick that piece of paper on the mirror in your bathroom where you brush your teeth. Tomorrow morning when you are brushing your teeth pinpoint a time in your day when you can spend ten minutes in the classroom of silence. If at all possible, stop by your church. It is probably empty and quiet for most of the day. I know we can pray anywhere, but there is something mystical and powerful about entering into the presence of God in His house.

I challenge you to take a few moments with your God each day. Enter into the classroom of silence. Sit with the Divine Architect and together design something wonderful. Visit with the Divine Navigator and plot a course to unchartered territories. Sit with God and dream some dreams.

Once you are in the classroom of silence, if you can muster the courage to ask the big question and the patience to listen to the silent murmurings of your heart, He will lead you. You may not hear any voices, or see any wonders, but He will lead you. Nothing is surer. And then, your life will become a passionate and enthusiastic adventure.

Forget about trying to put together a Master Plan for your life… for your happiness. Start looking for The Master's Plan for your life… for your happiness.

If you are willing, little by little, step by step, He will reveal a plan, and in that plan your deep gladness will unite with the world's deep need. Only then will you taste the holy contentment that our very beings never stop yearning for.

Get to know The Shepherd. He will lead you to green pastures… He will restore your soul… Your cup will overflow…

If you would like to order additional copies of this book, are interested in writing to the author, wish to receive his newsletter, would like information about his speaking engagements or would like to invite him to speak to your group, please address all correspondence to:

THE MATTHEW KELLY FOUNDATION

2330 KEMPER LANE
CINCINNATI, OH 45206
United States of America
www.matthewkelly.org